21 FIRSTS:

A NEW PARENT'S GUIDE TO THE MOMENTS THAT MATTER

From First Cries To First Steps, How To Thrive Through Your Baby's Earliest Milestones

By:

SWAPNA DAS

Clever Fox® PUBLISHING

Chennai • Bangalore

CLEVER FOX PUBLISHING
Chennai, India

Published by CLEVER FOX PUBLISHING 2025

ISBN: 978-93-6707-096-3

Gratitude

With deepest gratitude, I bow to you, Guru Ji, Sadguru Shri Aadinath, for your boundless blessings, unwavering guidance, and the light you bring into my life.

Dedication

I dedicate this book to my Mother and Father, without whom I would not be here. I am deeply grateful for their unwavering support, given in the best way they could. Love you, **Mummy and Achhan**!

I dedicate this book to **Guru Maa**, who guided me through a critical stage of my spiritual journey, giving me new direction and a new life. Maa, I will be forever grateful to you. It is because of you, and the hope you instilled in me, that this book came into being. Thank you, Maa! Love you, Maa!

Last but not least, I dedicate this book to my husband, **Sudeep**, my son, **Soham**, and to **myself**. As a family, we have journeyed together through life's ups and downs, emerging stronger. Soham, thank you for being in my life, for teaching me valuable lessons, and for filling my days with precious moments. Sudeep, thank you for your early insights during the editing of this book and for walking beside me every step of the way.

Thank you, Sudeep and Soham — I love you!

CONTENTS

PART I

THE FOUNDATION, SURVIVING THE FIRST WEEK

Summary: This part dives into the physical trauma, emotional vulnerability, and utter bewilderment many new mothers feel, but few dare to put into words. It's where the dream of serene, glowing motherhood collides with the messy reality of bodily aches, newborn cries, and the dawning awareness that *you* were born that day too, as a mother.

What to Expect:

- The contrast between fantasy and reality during childbirth
- The disorientation of first-time feeding
- A mother being born alongside her baby

CHAPTERS:

1

FIRST CRY: WHEN YOU REALISE YOU'RE A PARENT

They say the first cry of your baby is the most beautiful sound you'll ever hear.

They do not, however, tell you that you might hear it while lying flat on your back in a freezing operating theatre, wearing an open hospital gown that does nothing for your dignity, wondering who exactly decided to slice you open without fully looping you in.

As I was being taken to the operating theatre, I looked at the huge lights on the ceiling, thinking of those movie scenes where they show the red light on the OT door. I almost laughed, until the next wave of excruciating labour pain reminded me I'd been enduring this for over 5 hours. I screamed… "Mummyyyyyy…."

The operating theatre was nothing like the soft-lit birthing suites in glossy pregnancy magazines. Instead, it resembled a cross between a science lab and an aircraft hangar: cold, bright, humming with equipment, and filled with people talking in rapid-fire medical shorthand as though I wasn't the main event. Steel trays were lined with mysterious instruments (which I later realised were just fancy scissors and oversized tweezers), and the faint smell of antiseptic clung to the air like bad perfume.

The plan, apparently, was an **emergency C-section**. My husband and my mother were informed. I… was not.

Women's empowerment? My body, my decisions? Apparently, those concepts had taken a short tea break that day.

No one asked if I wanted an epidural or full anesthesia. It was as if some silent medical group chat had already decided for me. Then came the epidural, a cold, sharp invasion that made me momentarily forget I had agreed to be a mother. And then the numbness. No pain, but full sensory awareness. I could see everything. Hear everything. And yet, at that moment, I was strangely calm.

The doctor made a tiny incision and asked, "How are you feeling, Swapna?" I just nodded and said, "I'm okay." Seconds later, she lifted a pair of tiny feet into the air. "Here is your son." And she announced the birth time.

My first reaction? **Why?**

I had secretly wished for a girl baby all along. Then came the realisation: ***My son. My baby.*** And then… oh dear, they'd taken him away already.He was whisked off for cleaning while I lay there like an experiment cut open, all at the mercy of these people around me, the doctor started stitching me back together.

Or so I thought.

Midway through stitching me back together, the nurse urgently called the doctor to the cleaning station. My stomach and stitches were left mid-operation while she rushed off. I lay there thinking: *Will I ever be put together again? Will I stand? Is my baby okay?*

Moments later I learned why: my son had been born with the umbilical cord wrapped around his neck. He had turned purple. He wasn't breathing. The doctor revived him. And then I heard it, the much-glorified **first cry**.

I wish I could say it was pure magic. Honestly, my head was spinning, my heart was pounding, and my body felt like it had been in a bar fight with gravity.

Back in my hospital room, they placed my son in my arms. In movies, this is when the mother beams, angels sing, and everyone cries happy tears. In my case, I was struggling to hold this tiny snow-blob without dropping him. My hands were trembling, my arms aching, and my nausea building. I smiled weakly… I gave my baby back to my mother and I yelled..I want to throw up..

When I stood up, I was hit by a tidal wave of pain. My inside organs felt as though they might stage a dramatic escape through the nearest exit. I took three small steps before hurling into a strategically placed bowl. I thought my stitches would come off… my brain would explode..What pain should I cry for..

The nurse cleaned me up like I was a baby myself, and I crawled back to bed in defeat.

REFLECTIONS & LESSONS, FIRST CRY

- Birth doesn't always look like the movies, and that's okay.
- You may not feel the instant magic everyone talks about; sometimes survival comes first.
- Your first act as a parent might be… not dropping the baby while you're about to vomit. And that's still love.
- There are plenty of guides for pregnancy. But no one really prepares you for the baby. Or the version of *you* that is born with them. You are here to become the mother your child needs, not the one society paints, or books prescribe.

2

FIRST FEEDING, GUILT: NOURISHMENT, BONDING

Motherhood waits for no pain. My baby wanted milk.

The milk production department in my body had apparently gone on strike.

And the baby kept wailing. No milk. Nature's back up. Try on the other side…I heard someone guiding me.. Nope. Maybe it's the stress. Try again in an hour.

Still nothing. The dairy had downed its shutters.

The cries of my hungry newborn felt like tiny daggers of guilt stabbing me in the chest. The nurses and relatives offered endless advice: "Hold him like this… feed him like this… no, not like that."

I wept in silence.

At some point in the night, the nurse finally gave him formula. Bless her.

By morning, the paediatrician arrived with an encyclopedia's worth of explanations about milk production, latching, and breast pumps. I had never even *heard* of a breast pump. Still, we bought the best quality one and tried. It didn't work. The doctor continued to encourage me to try, reminding me that "breast is best."

My husband and mother took turns walking him up and down the hospital corridor to calm him so I could rest. By the second day, his voice had started to change from all the crying. We finally tried the Lactogen formula, and my son stopped crying. The relief of seeing him satisfied and sleeping peacefully was indescribable.

At night, as he slept beside me in the cradle, I stood holding my bloated belly, walked to him and looked at him. That was our first real moment. He stared at the ceiling with half opened eyes, as if trying to figure out where he was and I looked at him with all the love in my heart.

I bent over his cradle, my voice barely a whisper but my chest on fire.

"I'm sorry I couldn't feed you,"

I breathed, the words tasting like shame.

The guilt didn't just sit quietly; it clawed at me. It made me angry at my own body for betraying me, furious that something so natural was impossible for me, and bitter at the endless voices telling me I was failing him.

Every tiny cry felt like an accusation I couldn't answer.

I pitied him for having a mother who couldn't give him what the world said was best, and I pitied myself for carrying that wound day after day.

It wasn't just guilt anymore, it was a storm, and it took me months to crawl out from under it.

Reflections & Lessons, First Feeding

- Feeding your baby is about love and nourishment, not the method.
- You may not produce milk, and that's ok. Breastfeeding is beautiful, but not the only way to nourish your precious bundle. Your baby will thrive because of your love, not just your milk.
- You are not alone. Even when you feel like it. You have your baby guiding you what it needs.
- **Guilt doesn't have an expiry date, unless you give it one.** If you're waiting for it to magically vanish, spoiler: it won't. You have to actively decide to release it.
- You are not failing; you are mothering in the way your baby needs.

3

FIRST VACCINATION: WHEN YOU REALIZE YOUR BABY HAS TO BEAR SOME PAIN ON HIS OWN

As if the guilt over feeding wasn't enough, the universe decided to test me again, because apparently, motherhood is a full-time endurance game with no commercial breaks.

We soon had to face his first vaccinations.
The tiny needles looked **bigger than his entire thigh**, and for the record, that is not an exaggeration when you're holding a baby who is still basically the size of a water bottle.

The nurse asked me to hold him still. *Hold him still?!* My internal voice wanted to scream:
"Are you out of your mind? He's my baby, not a paperweight!"

Then came the jab.
He wailed, one of those deep, heart-splitting cries that makes you feel like you've single-handedly destroyed the concept of trust forever. I wailed too. We were a duet of despair, and I'm fairly sure the clinic waiting room still echoes with it.

Somewhere deep down, even through the sobs, I realised something that I wasn't ready to know: *there will always be pain he has to go through alone.*

I can't take the needle for him. I can't swap places. I can't shield him from every sting.
I can only stand beside him, be his safe place to collapse into, and whisper, *"It's over, it's over."*

Just when I thought the drama had peaked with the First Vaccination, the universe smirked and said, *"Oh, you think that was bad? Hold my coffee."*

I noticed it first in my baby's eyes, a faint yellow tint. At first, I told myself I was imagining it. New-mum paranoia, I thought. But by the next feed, the yellow wasn't just in his eyes. There was pus formation in his eyes. I was asking myself, one eye looks good, what is wrong with the other one?

Cue panic. Full-blown, all-caps PANIC.
This wasn't the "awww-look-he's-so-cute" kind of baby moment. This was me pondering *"Is my baby turning into a minion?"* at 3am while holding him up to the light like I was inspecting a produce at a supermarket.

The pediatrician confirmed it: Jaundice. Common in newborns, they said. Treatable, they said. No big deal, they said. Meanwhile, my brain had already written his medical autobiography and cast the Netflix adaptation.

We were sent home with instructions that read like a military operation:

- Sunlight therapy in measured doses.
- Feeding on a strict clock.
- Endless monitoring.

It wasn't glamorous. It wasn't cute. It was my mom again to the rescue for the first week. She would take him outside, sit on the stairs singing songs and let the sunlight do its miracle. I used to watch his skin under the morning sun like some over-caffeinated scientist. Every burp felt like progress. Every nap felt like borrowed time.

And still, the guilt was there, whispering, "Is this somehow your fault?" Because apparently motherhood comes with an in-built guilt soundtrack on repeat.

Thankfully, after days that felt like months, the yellow began to fade. The whites of his eyes returned to white. My breathing returned to something resembling normal. The doctor cleared him, and for the first time in what felt like forever, I allowed myself to believe we were okay.

But here's the thing about First Jaundice: it's not just about the bilirubin count. It's about the first time you realise your baby's health is a fragile little thread, and you're holding it with trembling hands.

Reflections & Lessons, First Guilt

- **Some pain you can't take away.** This is the brutal truth of parenting: you will watch them hurt and know you can't fix it at that moment. Your presence matters more than your ability to solve.
- **Needles are a metaphor for life.** They hurt, they're quick, and they leave a mark, but you heal. And so does your baby.
- **Medical checklists are grounding.** When emotions are flooding, having concrete steps to follow keeps you from drowning in "what-ifs."
- **Humour helps.** It may not make the jab hurt less, but it stops you from feeling like the jab is *your* personal parenting scorecard.
- **Be your baby's safe space.** Even when you can't take the pain, you can be the arms they trust to hold them right after.
- **Paranoia has its perks.** You might feel dramatic, but noticing small changes can be the difference between "caught early" and "caught too late."
- **Instructions = sanity.** When panic is high, having a list to tick off is oddly comforting. It gives you something to *do* besides spiralling.
- **Sunlight therapy is free, but it costs your peace of mind.** You will hover, you will second-guess, you will squint at their skin like you have X-ray vision.
- **Trust the boring answer.** Sometimes the doctor really does mean, "It's common, it'll pass." Not every crisis is a Netflix drama. (Even if it feels like one.)

- **You're already a guardian.** You don't need to be a doctor to protect your baby, you just need to notice, act, and show up every time.

4

FIRST EXCITEMENT: NAMING

As my strength returned, small bursts of excitement began to bloom. What should we name him? What clothes should I buy? How do I bathe this fragile being? How do I massage him? Thankfully, my mother answered many of these questions.

I'd hoped for a girl and already had a name picked. But when the doctor showed me my son, I was a bit disappointed as well. But when it came time to choose his name, our enthusiasm was at its peak, we were selecting something for him, something that would stay with him forever, even though he had no say in it yet. That thought brought me a little pressure too.

What if, as he grows up, he doesn't like the name we chose for him?

My husband got a print out which had baby boy names.. All from God's names to natures synonyms, to European names, to French names, to Greek God's names, to the names I had not even heard and few names in Sanskrit. The process was fun..the name Aditya, beautiful, but we already knew a couple of Aditya's..and what if we go to the United States and his short name will be "Adi" and everyone in his class would call him *"Adi- das", Das being our last name...* The thought kind of terrified us but we had to pick one name and we continued..

Then we discussed what if our son's name starts with a V..like Vijay..His roll number will be last.. He will sit in the exam hall last.. by the time the teacher checks the paper his paper will not get full attention.. Seriously..the kind of thoughts that come to mind is hilarious.

My husband, my mother, and I went through each one of them alphabetically until we landed on the name "**Soham**", all three of us unanimously agreed. It felt perfect, as if it had been waiting for him all along. We forgot to think further and put a full stop on name search. We were not tired, but the name was just perfect, beautiful and I imagined him calling Soham. It's a different story that I called him all his life by a different name.. As we are mandated to have one name for home and another for school and the outside world. Funny, isn't it!

Reflections & Lessons, First Excitement

- The first week is a blur of exhaustion, but small joys still bloom.
- Naming your child can feel like naming your heart, choose with love.
- Let excitement exist alongside exhaustion; both belong in the first week.

PART II

THE FOUNDATION, SURVIVING THE FIRST THREE MONTHS

Building the Bond – Surviving the First Three Months

Summary: They say there's no place like home. I disagree, there's no place quite like home *with a newborn*. It's a cross between a war zone and a royal court: constant demands, unpredictable eruptions, and at least one person (you) operating on zero sleep while pretending to be in charge.You shift into adjusting life with a newborn, the exhaustion, the guilt, and small joys. This is where bonding and breakdowns happen side-by-side.

What to Expect:

- The struggle of sleep and breastfeeding
- The reality of emotional recovery and mood swings
- First glimpses of joy through tiny milestones

CHAPTERS:

---

5. **First Night Home: Chaos Meets Crib**
6. **First Meltdown: Yours, Not The Baby's**
   Understanding postpartum emotions, father/partner stress, and asking for help
7. **First Routine: the Myth and the magic**
   Breastfeeding, bottle feeding, and learning what works for your baby, not the books.
8. **First Laughter: The Breakthrough Moment**
   Recognizing emotional milestones and the power of tiny affirmations in long sleepless nights.

5

FIRST NIGHT HOME: CHAOS MEETS CRIB

We stepped through the front door with our new baby, brimming with a strange cocktail of pride, fear, and exhaustion. This was our moment. We were a family.

We were greeted by a huge banner made by my husband glued-together A4 sheets that read:

"Welcome Home Son, Son's Mom and Mom's Mom"

It was sweet. It was touching. It was also a silent promise that this house was now officially run by the *smallest* member of the family. Ok, that also meant my husband could be creative if he wanted to. I wanted to ask why he hid his talent while we were dating, for my birthdays or the anniversaries. I kept quiet as I wanted to enjoy that moment.

Within minutes, we realised this was also the moment, life as we knew it, would never exist again.

The house felt both familiar and alien. The bed looked inviting, but so did the sofa, the floor, and even the laundry basket. Anything that could hold my collapsing body was fair game.

Meanwhile, my son expressed his opinion about his new home by screaming loudly enough to alert the neighbourhood dogs. Somewhere out there, a stray probably thought, "Yep, new human pup in the territory."

My emotions and workaholic mind spilled in every direction: Should I rest? Cook? Clean? Unpack the hospital bags? Write a thank-you card to the medical team for keeping me alive? Every thought was interrupted by either the baby crying, my stitches aching, or my mother bustling about the kitchen like a master chef on a mission.

Moms be blessed! Particularly moms of daughters. Particularly after the daughter's childbirth.

My mother was an absolute blessing, producing hot, fragrant, healing food at lightning speed. My husband, who had taken a few precious days off work (paternity leave wasn't really a thing then), was equally heroic, assembling furniture, fetching water, changing nappies, and Googling "How to swaddle without breaking my baby or marriage."

And yet, in the middle of all this help, I felt the sting of guilt. The Great Feeding Failure was still fresh in my mind. I wanted to enjoy the first night home, but the soundtrack in my head was: *You can't even feed him yourself.* That voice was as persistent as the baby's cries, and far less cute.

REFLECTIONS & LESSONS, FIRST NIGHT HOME

- **The first night home isn't peaceful, it's a welcome-home party thrown by chaos.** Forget candles and quiet. Expect noise, spills, and at least one existential crisis before midnight.
- **Accept all the help you can get, even if your pride protests.** This is not the moment to prove you can "do it all." You've just had major surgery (or labour). Let other people carry the laundry, hold the baby, or feed you like a sleepy baby bird.
- **You are allowed to feel grateful and guilty at the same time.** One does not cancel out the other. Motherhood comes with emotional two-for-one deals.
- **Your home will feel different.** It's the same walls, same furniture, but now it's Headquarters for Operation Keep the Baby Alive.
- **Food is a love language.** Healing food delivered at lightning speed by people who love you should be accepted without hesitation.
- **Guilt will gatecrash your first night.** Don't let it take the microphone. Your baby doesn't care about your feeding method as much as they care about your arms.
- **You don't have to 'do' anything special tonight.** You're already doing the most important job: being there.
- **Your bed will look like heaven… but you won't get to lie in it uninterrupted.** Adjust expectations early.

6

FIRST MELTDOWN: YOURS, NOT THE BABY'S

Determined to redeem myself after The Great Feeding Failure, I gave pumping one last heroic shot. And by "heroic," I mean a month of unproductive, joy-sucking, body-shaming effort that left me questioning why breast pumps don't come with free therapy sessions.

Finally, in a dramatic, Oscar-worthy moment, I hurled the pump into a cupboard and declared:

"That's it. We're done here."

I imagined triumphant applause. Instead, the cupboard door creaked shut in solidarity and my baby continued to cry for formula.

Our paediatrician suggested we track feedings and nappies, so we started a journal like the diligent new parents we wanted to be.

And yes, the first week's notes looked like NASA was monitoring a space launch: precise times, measurements, even smiley faces for "good feeds."

We also decided a cradle might make life easier. My mother laughed, "Not needed."
But we were next-gen parents, armed with Google, overconfidence, and the belief that *our* baby would love it.
Spoiler: he didn't.
He screamed the moment we put him down. Loudly. As if the cradle was a medieval torture device. We gave it away in record time.

Eight days after surgery, my stitches came out. I started to feel physically stronger. That's when I went into "organised mum" mode, buying a bathing mat, a massage mat, enough bottles to survive an apocalypse, a steriliser, and a flask to store warm water for night-time feeds. We all took turns preparing formulas so I could rest.

Physically, I was healing. Emotionally? I was unravelling like a ball of yarn in a kitten factory.

I snapped over everything:

- The TV volume being three decibels too loud.
- The feeding bottle sitting in the "wrong" spot on the kitchen counter.
- The audacity of anyone telling me to "rest more."

Back then, no one in my circle mentioned "postnatal depression." You were just told to "adjust", as if you were a slightly crooked picture frame.

And then it happened. My mum started packing to return to work.
One day, I screamed at my programmed robot husband over something small and the robot abandoned its programming, turned into Mr Smith from matrix, and he screamed back. I had a huge meltdown.

That was my breaking point.
I was sobbing. Snot dripping. Face blotchy. Hair wild. The kind of cry where you don't just make sound, you *leak emotions from every pore.*

And then it hit me: He was exhausted too.
We were two overtired humans, each silently convinced the other had it easier.

So when my mum suggested I go back with her to my hometown for a while, I said yes faster than a toddler spotting cake.

Reflections & Lessons, First Meltdown

- **Meltdowns are part of recovery, not proof of failure.** They're emotional pressure-release valves, and sometimes they save you from imploding.
- **Your partner is adjusting too; exhaustion is a shared language.** You're both learning, fumbling, and winging it. No one's holding the "How to Parent Without Losing Your Mind" manual because it doesn't exist.
- **Sometimes the bravest thing is to say "I need to go home."** Rest isn't weakness; it's fuel.

- **Cradles, breast pumps, and other "must-have" baby items are not marriage savers.** They're more like social experiments. Some work, some get sold on OLX.
- **Your anger isn't about the burp cloth.** It's about sleep deprivation, hormonal chaos, and a love so fierce it's overwhelming.
- **Don't measure your worth by your composure.** A good cry can be just as productive as a tidy house.
- **Humour is a survival skill.** If you can laugh about throwing a breast pump into a cupboard, you're doing okay.
- **Accept strategic retreats.** Going to your mum's isn't "running away"; it's choosing peace, extra hands, and someone who won't judge your messy bun.
- **The people who love you will understand.** And they'll make you tea while you cry.

7

FIRST ROUTINE: THE MYTH AND THE MAGIC

Back home, my mum arranged for a daily massage, heaven in human form. The kind that made me feel like melted butter in human skin. My body softened. My mind unclenched. My baby began cooing and smiling in that gummy, heart-melting way that makes you forgive every sleepless night.

I started talking to him regularly. Not just "goo-goo, gaa-gaa," but actual conversations:

"So, what do you think about the rising price of tomatoes?"
"Shall we have a bath now or later?"
"Did you just burp at me or was that applause?"

Slowly, he began to respond. Little coos. Tiny smiles. That "I'm pretending to understand you" look. It was our first real rhythm. Not quite a schedule, but something resembling a routine, the kind you feel more than you write down.

And then came the next parenting myth, whispered with authority by well-meaning relatives:

"Babies should lie on their tummy by the 40th day."

Mine didn't.
Not on the 40th day. Not on the 41st. Not even on the 45th.

With every visitor, the first question wasn't "How are you coping?" or "Do you need help?" No. It was:

> "Did your baby turn?"
> "When are you leaving?"
> "Oh, dear, your husband must be missing you!"
> "How is your husband surviving?"

And I'd politely smile, because that's what we're taught. Smile. Adjust. Pretend you're not silently planning a fake "baby on tummy" photoshoot with a doll just to make them stop asking.

The truth is, I realised routines are lovely… but they're not life-or-death. And no amount of neighbourly interrogation will change your baby's timeline.

REFLECTIONS & LESSONS, FIRST ROUTINE

- **Routines help, but they're not gospel.** A flexible flow that works for you beats a rigid clock set by a stranger's expectations.
- **Milestones are not a competition.** Your baby's pace is perfect, even if it makes relatives twitch.
- **Deflect unhelpful commentary with humour.** You don't owe anyone progress reports.

- **Connection matters more than checklists.** Eye contact, silly banter, and being present beat any "perfect" schedule.
- **Parenting myths are like bad forwarded WhatsApp messages.** Smile, nod, and ignore as needed.
- **Your baby's cues are your best guide.** Not the neighbour's advice, not the milestone chart.
- **Keep the joy in your routine.** The schedule is for you, the magic is for both of you.

8

FIRST LAUGHTER: THE BREAKTHROUGH MOMENT

One evening, while I was lying next to him making silly faces, my usual act in the "Mum's One-Woman Baby Comedy Show", I sneezed.
Not a polite little "achoo."
No, this was a full-bodied, dramatic, head-jerking, Oscar-worthy sneeze that could have startled the postman two streets away.

He froze for a second… eyebrows raised, mouth slightly open as if thinking: *What on earth was that, and can we keep it?*

And then, just like the sun breaking through storm clouds, he burst into the most joyful, musical belly laugh I'd ever heard. It wasn't just a sound. It was pure, fizzy happiness bubbling out of him.

Naturally, I did what any sane adult would do: I sneezed again.

He laughed harder, like his tiny ribs couldn't possibly contain it all.

That was it. Game on.

I kept sneezing in increasingly ridiculous ways.
A big dramatic wind-up sneeze.
A fake sneeze with jazz-hands.
A sneeze that sounded suspiciously like a goose in distress.

He laughed at *every single one*. That laugh, sharp little gasps mixed with squeals, rolled around the room, and my heart did cartwheels. For a moment I thought, "I should do a PhD on sneezing!"

Twenty sneezes later, we were both red-faced, giggling like lunatics. His little fists kept flying into the air like he was conducting the music of his own joy. Tears streamed down my cheeks, the happy kind.

And that's when it hit me: **this** is the magic of parenting. Not the milestones visitors obsess over. Not the charts and "by-this-age" checklists. It's in the unexpected, unplanned, and totally ridiculous moments where joy sneaks in and takes over.

That night of sneezes unlocked something in me.
I stopped obsessing over what we weren't doing "right" and started noticing what was working: he was fed, loved, clean, and, in his own time, happy.

Sometimes a laugh is more healing than a full night's sleep.
Sometimes it's the moment that makes you think: *I might actually be okay at this.*

REFLECTIONS & LESSONS, FIRST LAUGHTER

- **Laughter is therapy.** It melts the stress, silences the inner critic, and connects you instantly.
- **Tiny moments can carry you through hard weeks.** Sometimes a sneeze beats a milestone.
- **Joy is never scheduled.** It bursts in uninvited and turns an ordinary day extraordinary.
- **Let silliness be part of your parenting toolkit.** It soothes, bonds, and teaches your child that home is a safe place for joy.
- **A baby's laughter is contagious medicine.** Don't ration it. Indulge in it daily.
- **Happiness isn't in "what's next."** It's in the giggle right in front of you.

PART III

BUILDING THE BOND, 3 TO 6 MONTHS

Summary: You shift into adjusting life with a newborn, the exhaustion, the guilt, and small joys. This is where bonding and breakdowns happen side-by-side. The first "Ah-goo" felt like a love letter in baby language. We mimicked each other for hours. Then came hair-pulling. And grabbing. And the art of toy-to-head combat.

We started using semi-solids. Cerelac was a hit… until spitting it out became the main sport.

What to Expect:

- The struggle of sleep and breastfeeding
- The reality of emotional recovery and mood swings
- First glimpses of joy through tiny milestones

CHAPTERS:

9

FIRST SOUND PLAY: BABBLING BEGINS

Somewhere around the third month, my baby started making sounds that were clearly meant to be the opening lines of our lifelong conversation.

Not random cries anymore, no, these were actual coos, gurgles, and vowel sounds that felt like secret codes.

We'd sit facing each other, staring intently as though about to discuss the mysteries of the universe, and he'd start:

"Ah-gooo."

I'd reply with perfect mimicry:

"Ah-gooo."

He'd grin, wide-eyed, as if to say: *Finally! A grown-up who speaks my language.*

And so it began: the Great Babbling Duets of 2004.

To an outsider, it might have sounded like a deranged echo chamber. To me, it was magic, our private, wordless dialogue, a sacred language of love, trust, and nonsense syllables that somehow made more sense than most adult conversations.

Of course, these heart-melting sessions came with occupational hazards. His tiny hands, which had previously been innocent, flailing accessories, suddenly developed a magnetic attraction to my hair. My curls became his ropes, and he pulled with the dedication of a pirate hoisting sails.
Soon, his grasp expanded to anything within reach, my clothes, my necklace, my earrings and *yes, mums, one firm tug can turn a sweet little earring hole into a permanent "statement piece".*

Sometimes, mid-coo, he'd yank my hair so hard I'd involuntarily contribute my own sound effect: *"Ow-gooo."*
He'd giggle. I'd forgive him. Because that's the power of your baby's first conversations, even when they hurt, they're still somehow perfect.

Reflections & Lessons, First Sound Play

- These coos and gurgles are your earliest conversations. They're telling you, "I see you. I hear you. I know you're my person."
- Talk back, even if you sound ridiculous. To your baby, you're not being silly; you're speaking their native tongue.
- Your face is the first "screen" they'll ever watch. Keep it animated, warm, and fully tuned in.

- Avoid dangling earrings unless you want free "piercing upgrades." And rethink necklaces too, unless you enjoy playing "tug of war" with your neck.
- This is the foundation of language. You're not just playing; you're literally wiring your baby's brain for speech and communication.
- Hair is not just hair. It's a baby-approved handlebar. Plan accordingly.

10

FIRST SEMI-SOLIDS: TINY BITES, BIG MOMENTS

By the fourth month, the paediatrician suggested we start semi-solids.

If you've never been to the baby food aisle in an Indian supermarket, imagine this:

A wall of cheerful packaging yelling promises like:

- **"Complete Nutrition!"**
- **"Gentle on Baby's Tummy!"**
- And my personal favourite: **"Helps Your Baby Sleep Through the Night!"** *(Lies. All lies.)*

We kept it simple and went with Cerelac.

My son took to it immediately, opening his mouth like a baby bird who had just spotted the worm delivery van.

A few spoonfuls in, he made a startling discovery: **spitting it out was way more fun than swallowing.**

The sheer artistry with which he could project Cerelac across a room was almost impressive. Almost.

Books will tell you: *"Feed until the baby seems full."*

Which would be great advice if babies came with a blinking **FULL** light on their foreheads. Mine didn't.

Sometimes he'd stop after three polite spoonfuls, like a little prince saying, *"Thank you, I'm done now, you may clear the table."*

Other times, he'd eat like a tiny sumo wrestler preparing for a championship match.

And then there were the curveballs: eating loads, looking satisfied... and then crying as though I'd personally ruined his life.

That's when I realised: feeding isn't just about filling a tummy. It's about mood, timing, teething, growth spurts, planetary alignment, and some mysterious baby code only they understand.

Reflections & Lessons, First Semi-Solids

- **First foods are more about discovery than nutrition.** The first month is about learning tastes, textures, and "spoon protocol."
- **Mess is part of the menu.** If it's not on their cheeks, eyebrows, and your shirt, did they even eat?
- **Ignore packaging promises.** That "sleep through the night" line is marketing poetry, not a scientific guarantee.

- **Let them lead the pace.** Some days they'll be a bottomless pit. Other days, they'll treat food like a passing hobby.
- **Texture matters.** That face they make when they taste something new? That's baby Yelp. Take notes.
- **Patience is an ingredient.** You'll need just as much of it as the actual food.
- **Cerelac on the wall? Normal.** On the ceiling? Still normal. On the neighbour's cat? Maybe close the window next time.

11

FIRST ROLL OVER: STRENGTH IN MOTION

One ordinary day, I bathed him, dressed him in his cutest romper, the one that made him look like he'd just stepped off a baby fashion runway, and laid him gently on his back.
I stepped away to make tea.
Seconds later, I heard a triumphant little grunt.

I rushed back, and there he was… on his tummy.
My baby had rolled over!

I squealed like I'd just won the lottery, complete with ridiculous arm flapping and possibly some squeaky noises that only dogs could hear. Naturally, I assumed it was a fluke. So I placed him back on his back.

Nope.
Like a tiny gymnast, he rolled over again, this time faster.
I tried again.

Same thing.
I repeated the experiment three times (in the name of science, of course), and each time he nailed it with smug baby confidence.

The "immobile newborn" era was officially over.
I no longer had a still, predictable baby.
I had a rolling machine, a rolling machine with zero awareness of furniture edges, electrical cords, or the fact that Mum had not yet had a baby-proofed the world.

It was exciting, terrifying, and slightly exhausting, all at once.

Reflections & Lessons, First Roll Over

- Milestones are mini-miracles, celebrate them loud. Even if it's "just rolling," it's your baby's first act of mobility. This is huge for them, and for you.
- Never underestimate the speed of progress (or the reach of tiny hands). Today's roll is tomorrow's crawl, and the day after that? Scaling furniture like a mountaineer.
- Floor time is your new best friend, and your new workout. You'll find yourself lunging, stretching, and diving like an Olympic goalkeeper to save them from trouble.
- Baby-proofing starts now. If it's sharp, small, or dangerous, move it. If it's expensive, *definitely* move it.
- Video it. This is one of those moments you'll want to replay forever, preferably with an over-the-top sports commentary soundtrack. We did not have smart phones to capture these moments.

12

FIRST TOOTH: THE TINY ARRIVAL THAT CHANGES EVERYTHING

One day, while I was holding him, I spotted it, a tiny white bump peeking out of his lower gums.
Teething had arrived.
Another milestone. Another challenge. Another test of my patience.

In theory, it's cute.
In reality, it's like living with a tiny, drooly dragon.

He gnawed on *everything*, his fingers, my fingers, toys, the mattress edge, my shoulder (usually while pretending to cuddle), and occasionally things I wish he hadn't discovered.
We tried teething toys, he preferred toast.
We tried cold spoons, he preferred gnawing on his toys.
We tried distraction, he preferred crying.

And with teething came sleepless nights.
The kind where you try every trick in the book - lullabies, cuddles, swings, whispered pep talks and nothing works.

Until… we found our holy grail: night-time bike rides.
Yes, really.
We'd wrap him up, strap him safely, and ride through the cool night air. He'd be asleep in minutes. The neighbours probably thought we'd lost it, cycling around the block at midnight with a bundled-up baby, but it worked.

That's how we survived teething: one breezy, slightly eccentric, night ride at a time.

Reflections & Lessons, First Tooth

- Teething is a patience marathon. Stock up on comfort items, for the baby and yourself.
- Sleep solutions can be unconventional. Try what works, not just what's in the books. If it's safe and your baby sleeps, you're winning.
- Drool is now a lifestyle. Bibs aren't optional. Neither is a good laundry routine.
- Everything is a teething toy. EVERYTHING. Prepare accordingly.
- Sometimes survival looks like riding a bike at midnight. If it works, it works, parenting isn't a performance, it's survival mixed with love.
- Humour helps. In the middle of the teething fog, being able to laugh about your baby's "tiny dragon" phase keeps you sane.

PART IV

GROWING TOGETHER, 6 TO 8 MONTHS

Summary: This is exactly the stage where babies transform from sweet, stationary bundles into mobile, mischievous chaos machines… and parents realise they need eyes in the back of their heads. It's also where motherhood starts to feel more intuitive.

What to Expect:

- First sounds, solids, sitting up and rolling
- The power of baby-led play and communication
- The parent-child bond deepening through routine and mess

CHAPTERS:

13

FIRST WORDS: COMMUNICATION BEFORE LANGUAGE

By six months, my baby was starting to talk… well, *his* version of talk.

No dictionary on earth could translate it, but I could. I was fluent in Babble-ese.

His "words" came with matching facial expressions and hand gestures. If he yelled "Ba-ba-ba" while smacking a toy against the floor, I knew exactly which "ba-ba" he meant.

He had a sound for excitement, a sound for "pick me up now," and one for "how dare you leave the room without me."
And just like any passionate speaker of their native tongue, he did *not* appreciate being ignored.

The real magic was the way he looked straight into my eyes when "talking", as if trying to download his thoughts directly into my brain without waiting for the whole "learning to speak" update.

Sometimes I'd babble back just to see what he'd do. And without fail, his whole face would light up like I'd just told him the best baby joke in history.
We weren't just communicating, we were *collaborating*.

Reflections & Lessons, First Words

- Listen beyond the sounds. Babies speak with their eyes, their hands, their wiggly toes, and occasionally, their eyebrows.
- Babble back. Even if it's nonsense, it teaches them that communication is a two-way street. Plus, you'll feel ridiculous, in the best way.
- Learn their personal "dictionary." "Ba-ba" at 6 a.m. may mean "bottle" while "ba-ba" at 6 p.m. could mean "Where's the cat?"
- Don't rush the real words. These early babbles are precious, they're the raw, unfiltered soundtrack of your baby discovering their voice.
- You don't just hear their words. You feel them. Some messages are delivered straight to your heart, bypassing the ears entirely.

14

FIRST SLEEP-THROUGH: MYTH OR MIRACLE?

People love to tell you:

"Once babies crawl, they'll sleep better."
"Once they start solids, you'll sleep through the night."

My son heard these and decided to treat them as personal challenges.

Crawling marathons? Still woke up.
A belly full of dinner? Still woke up.
Bath, massage, lullabies, prayers to the sleep gods? Still. Woke. Up!

There was nothing "wrong" with him, he just liked midnight parties.

I'm convinced he was mentally running a baby TED Talk series in his cot at 3 a.m., titled *Why Sleep Is Overrated or Play time is all the time or These adults need to chill...*

By now, I'd stopped asking the paediatrician for magical sleep answers. I accepted that my baby was a night owl. A philosopher. Possibly writing a baby version of *War and Peace* in his head while I counted imaginary sheep.

REFLECTIONS & LESSONS, FIRST SLEEP-THROUGH

- Sleeping "through the night" is an urban legend in baby-land. If someone tells you their baby did it at 3 weeks, smile politely and change the subject.
- Let go of the idea that sleep is a milestone to conquer. Babies don't read parenting books.
- Your baby's rhythm is unique. Comparing is a shortcut to frustration and self-doubt.
- Survival mode is okay. If the whole house is getting some rest, even in shifts, you're doing fine.
- Night feeds, night chats, night cuddles, they won't last forever. One day you might even miss them… though right now, you'd pay someone good money to make them stop.

15

FIRST BIG MESS: EMBRACING IMPERFECTION

With mobility came mealtime independence. I started offering him bite-sized food.

His approach? Pick it up. Inspect it. Throw it on the floor. Pick it up again. Eat it anyway.
(We are clearly raising a scientist.)

Then came The Mango Day.

His first taste of mango turned into a full-body sensory workshop. The high chair, the floor, his hair, my hair, even the cat, *all mango-ed*. It looked like a tropical fruit festival had exploded in my kitchen.

He grinned like he'd invented joy. I stared at the chaos and briefly considered mopping as a full-time career.

Instead, I decided this was going to be a learning moment. After eating, I'd hand him the empty bowl and guide him to put dropped food in the trash. He thought it was a game, *Mum's School of Cleaning* was born.

The mess didn't stop that day... but my attitude toward it did.

REFLECTIONS & LESSONS, FIRST BIG MESS

- Mess means progress. Babies learn by touching, squishing, and yes, dropping.
- Forget spotless. Your home should look *lived in*, not like a furniture showroom.
- Involve them in clean-up early. Even if they "help" by putting one spoon in the bin and wearing another as a hat, you're building lifelong habits.
- Mess is sensory learning. It's science, art, and play all rolled into one very sticky package.
- Choose washable over perfect. From bibs to rugs to your own shirt, assume mango is forever.
- One day, you'll miss the mess. Not *all* of it, but you might look at a spotless dining area and think: "Remember when this room smelled like mango puree?"

16

FIRST DISLOCATION: WHEN PLAY TURNS PAINFUL

One morning, after his usual royal post-massage glow, the kind that makes him look like he's ready to star in a luxury spa brochure, I left him lounging on the bed to fetch warm bathwater.

Normally, he'd crawl right back to me like a baby homing pigeon. But that day… nothing.

No rustling.
No giggling.
No tiny "I'm-about-to-pounce-on-you" squeal.

I froze mid-step.
Something's wrong.

I grabbed his favourite building block, our sacred crawling bribe and held it out like a baited fishing hook.
He reached forward… with one hand.

And then… stopped.

No crying.
No fussing.
Just… *wrong*.

And that's when my mum's radar went into high alert!
Because if motherhood teaches you anything, it's this:
Tears you can deal with. Silence is suspicious.

I called my husband:

"Something's not right. We're going to the doctor."

To be clear, it wasn't the calm "we should probably get that checked" kind of voice.
It was the "if you don't meet me at the hospital, I'm changing the Netflix password" kind of voice.

We drove like it was an action movie chase scene, except instead of screeching tyres and car flips, my baby sat quietly in his car seat holding a block, looking like nothing was wrong.
Meanwhile, my internal monologue was doing cartwheels:

What if he's broken something? What if it's nerve damage? What if I have to bubble-wrap him forever? Can babies live in padded hamster balls?

The paediatrician took one look and sent us straight to an orthopaedic specialist.
Quick check. A small smile. And then, in the most casual voice imaginable:

"His elbow is dislocated."

Sorry… *what*?
Do you mean his elbow, the bendy thing between his adorable baby hand and his chubby shoulder roll? The elbow that has barely been on this planet for half a year?

Apparently, yes.
The most likely culprit? Swinging during play. That sweet, giggly "wheee!" arm swing the one that made me feel like Fun Mum of the Year had actually popped his elbow out.

The doctor popped it back into place, while I tried not to pass out, then handed him a pen.
My son reached for it with both hands like nothing had ever happened.
Meanwhile, I was already mentally drafting a 3,000-word essay titled: *I Am the Worst Mother Alive.*

And that's how I learned that even joy has boundaries.
And that babies can terrify you to your core and then immediately ask for snacks.

REFLECTIONS & LESSONS, FIRST DISLOCATION

- **Trust your gut.** If something feels off, act. You don't need visible tears for proof.
- **Babies are suspiciously resilient.** They can survive a dislocation and be back to playing five minutes later. You will not recover as quickly.

- **Silence can be scarier than screaming.** A quiet baby can mean trouble, or that they're decorating the wall with yoghurt. Both require immediate attention.
- **Play is not risk-free.** Even the "fun" stuff needs limits. Save the circus tricks for after they learn to say, "Don't do that, Mum."
- **You will age five years in five minutes.** Accept it. Add collagen to your diet.
- **Forgive yourself.** Parenthood comes with a guarantee: at some point, something will happen on your watch. What matters is how quickly you step in.

PART V

THE LEAP, 8 TO 12 MONTHS, BABY TURNS ONE

Summary: "In watching them take their first steps, you realise you've been learning to let go." From first steps to first "No's," this stage is a whirlwind of independence, surprises, and heart-tugging goodbyes to babyhood. It's as much your milestone as theirs, a celebration of growth, resilience, and the bond you've built in the first year.

What to Expect:

- Walking, falling, growing, testing
- First birthday, separation, and identity shift
- Beginning to let go

CHAPTERS:

---

17. **First Steps: A New Kind of Freedom**
    Understanding the emotional and physical milestones of walking, for your baby and for you as a parent.
18. **First "No": Boundaries Begin Here**
    The beginning of independence, testing limits, and setting kind but firm boundaries while nurturing trust and confidence.
19. **First Time They Scare You: The Panic Moments**
    From falls to mystery rashes, how to respond with clarity (even when your heart is racing).
20. **First Birthday: Celebrating Survival**
    Planning a celebration that honors growth, not perfection, and reflecting on how much you've evolved too.
21. **First Goodbye to Babyhood: The Moment You Realize They're Growing**
    Processing pride and nostalgia as your baby turns one, and learning to embrace the evolving version of you.

17

FIRST STEPS: A NEW KIND OF FREEDOM

As my baby mastered crawling, he began to pull himself up and try standing, and by the seventh month, he was already doing it with ease.
All those massages he was receiving, yes, the kind that could bankrupt you if given at a spa had built his strength, and before long, he was standing confidently and walking by holding onto the wall for support.

That's when I got him a simple walker.

But even without the walker, he had his own ideas.
He'd grab a chair, push it across the room like a tiny old man with a Zimmer frame, and reach wherever he wanted. The walker only made him faster, my hallway became his personal Formula 1 track.

The sound of those little plastic wheels on tile? Imagine the ominous hum of an approaching villain in a horror movie, but cuter. I'd be in the kitchen, hear that faint rumble, and know I had five seconds before he appeared in the doorway with a grin that said: *Yes, I am about to cause chaos. And no, you can't stop me.*

To support his growing curiosity and also to stop him from rearranging the contents of every drawer, I stuck colourful, informative charts on the walls. Fruits, vegetables, vehicles, household items, a mini-encyclopaedia right there in the hallway.

As he glided past them, we'd call out the names together.
I'd say "banana!" and he'd give me a look like: *Sure Mum, but have you considered pulling down the curtain rod instead?*

It became our learning game.
I also kept toys at his reach so he could explore as he wanted, which, in practice, meant every room looked like a small-scale toy shop had exploded.

We had just one rule from the beginning: **We play with toys, then we clean up.**
Did he follow it? Of course not.
At least not until I turned it into a song with exaggerated dance moves. Then suddenly cleaning became "fun", which lasted about six minutes before he wandered off mid-chorus.

By eight months, he began speaking simple words, and his vocabulary was increasing. By nine months, he was taking small independent steps.

By the tenth month, he had fully mastered walking, which is the polite way of saying he had fully mastered escaping at top speed while laughing manically over his shoulder.

REFLECTIONS & LESSONS, FIRST STEPS

- **First steps are emotional, they're also the first small steps away from you.** You cheer like they've just landed on the moon, then cry because they're walking away from your arms.
- **Walking is freedom, for them. Cardio for you.** Forget the gym. Just try catching a toddler with a stolen TV remote.
- **Baby-proof like your sanity depends on it.** Because it does. If it's sharp, fragile, valuable, or edible-but-not-edible, move it *now*.
- **Turn clean-up into a ritual.** Even if they only "help" by handing you one block before running off with the other 49.
- **Walking changes the parenting game.** The house suddenly has "zones", the Safe Zone, the Danger Zone, and the Zone Where He Just Was But Is Now Missing.
- **Celebrate the wobble.** It's proof of progress, courage, and sheer determination in a tiny body.

18

FIRST "NO": BOUNDARIES BEGIN HERE

He had gained independence, and with that, a new level of courage.

I even let him approach the stairs, where he learned to climb up and down safely. Yes, I hovered behind him like a stunt double in a toddler action movie, ready to catch him if he went off-script.

Now came the stage where my baby started testing my patience, and doing it with a charming, *Oscar-winning* smile. He understood my instructions perfectly:

- Not to go outside.
- Not to climb the stairs unsupervised.
- Not to throw things from the balcony like an amateur Olympic shot-putter.

But he also understood something else, how to test the limits. And in doing so, he tested me, my boundaries, my breath, my patience… and possibly my blood pressure.

He'd flash that mischievous grin, the one that said *"I know the rules, and I am about to break them in the most delightful way possible"*, and take off with his walker, knowing very well he was faster than me. Especially if the main or balcony door was open.

I watched his problem-solving skills bloom. He learned to push chairs to reach high places, and completely ignored my firm commands to "Wait!" or "Stop!"
In fact, I'm convinced that "Stop" in toddler language translates to:

Yes. Go faster. Do it now. And laugh while doing it.

So I shifted tactics.

I began gently saying:

- "No, thank you."
- "We'll go out in the evening."
- "Let's get down now, we'll get 'owy'."

At first, even these didn't help.
So I tried something else: distraction and redirection, the Jedi mind trick of parenting.
If he made a beeline for the balcony, I'd suddenly remember we had to look for his favourite ball. If he attempted to climb a chair, I'd gasp and say, "Oh no! Did I hear the toy truck calling your name?"

Eventually, I changed my entire routine so I could be around him like a quiet bodyguard - always alert, always close.

It was exhausting. He was fast, determined, and endlessly curious. But my mother's protective instincts were stronger. I simply couldn't let any harm come to him.

And so, I learned that parenting is less about shouting "No!" from the kitchen, and more about turning into a full-time undercover security agent with lightning reflexes.

REFLECTIONS & LESSONS, FIRST "NO"

- Boundaries aren't just rules, they're relationship builders. The goal isn't to win every battle, it's to keep trust while keeping them safe.
- "No" works better with redirection than confrontation. Offer a better option. A shiny distraction beats a flat-out refusal.
- Toddlers have a PhD in testing limits. Your job is to stay calm, even when you feel like a bouncer at a rock concert.
- Your calm is more persuasive than your volume. Shouting might get immediate compliance, but a gentle, consistent tone builds long-term respect.
- Protective instincts are exhausting, but priceless. You will never regret shadowing them, even if it means eating lunch in three-minute intervals.
- Humour saves the day. Laugh at their antics, quietly, so they don't think its approval, it's the only way to survive the "boundary-testing" years.

19

FIRST TIME THEY SCARE YOU: THE PANIC MOMENTS

As I tried my best to keep him safe, he occasionally fell, small tumbles when he lost balance, little stumbles that ended with a surprised face and a quick cuddle.

But one moment still makes my heart race.

My husband was getting ready to leave for work. Our son, seated in his walker, saw the door slightly open. In a flash, and I mean *superhuman baby speed*, he dashed towards it.

The walker gave him the illusion of freedom and the reality of wheels.
He couldn't balance the speed and tumbled forward with it.

I saw it happen.

In slow motion.

But I couldn't reach him in time. I couldn't be the super girl/mom at that moment.

The sound of the fall.. that soft thud followed by a split-second pause.. sent a chill down my spine. I froze.

Was he hurt?
Where did he land?
Is there blood?
Where is the damn ice pack?!
Do I even remember how to breathe?!

I ran to him. He was crying. That gut-punching, red-faced cry that says: *"That was terrifying, and I'm not okay until you hold me."* I picked him up and did the only thing I could do.. I held him. I rocked him. I whispered, again and again, "You're okay. You're okay. Mama's here. You're safe."

I washed his face. I gave him a cold pack, which he promptly threw across the room like a rebellious mini athlete. I carried him for what felt like an hour, even though it was probably twenty minutes.

Finally, he slept. Peacefully. As if nothing had happened.

I, on the other hand, aged five years in those twenty minutes.

That moment was enough for me to make a firm, irrevocable decision:

The walker had to go. Out. Gone. Banned. Never again.

He recovered within minutes, unfazed, unbothered, ready to explore again like a tiny gladiator who just shook off a training injury.

But I didn't forget that fall.

I never will.

Reflections & Lessons, First Panic Moments

- You can't prevent every fall. But you can be the softest place to land.
- Sometimes, the one who needs the longest recovery is you. Babies bounce back. Mothers replay the fall in high definition for weeks.
- The walker giveth and the walker taketh away. Freedom is great. Until it becomes speed… without brakes.
- Trust your reaction. When something feels *off*, act. Even if you overreact. Especially if you overreact. That's what instincts are for.
- Calm presence trumps panic. Your stillness will teach them how to self-soothe. (Even if you're internally screaming.)
- You'll question everything. "Should I have seen it coming?" "Should I bubble-wrap the entire house?" "Should I live inside a padded room with him until he's five?" The answer is no… but also yes.
- You don't need to be perfect. You just need to be there. Present. Open arms. Steady hands. Whispering love into tiny ears.

- Walkers: approach with extreme caution. Or better yet, consider early retirement. They're training wheels *and* chaos on wheels.
- Write it down. These are the moments that feel terrifying now… but one day, you'll tell this story and smile. Maybe even laugh.

20

FIRST BIRTHDAY: CELEBRATING SURVIVAL

As the days filled with exploration, messes, and endless photo memories, we suddenly realised something, it was nearly his first birthday.

And with it came a different kind of reflection.

Should we celebrate?
Whom do we invite?
He won't even remember this day… So why celebrate at all?
Just for society's sake?

At first, my practical brain whispered, *"Skip it. Save the money for diapers and a stronger coffee machine."*

But then my heart whispered louder, *"This isn't just his milestone… it's ours too."*

This wasn't only about marking his first year of life.

It was about marking our first year of survival, the year we were reborn as a mother, a father, a family.

We had grown alongside him.
We had evolved into responsible(ish) parents.
We had learned to function on less sleep than a college student during exam week.
We had mastered the fine art of catching vomit mid-air.
We laughed, cried, failed spectacularly, and tried again.

He had taught us patience, usually tested right before dinner or any meal as he would want to poop at the same time, presence and joy, usually involving mango pulp, peek-a-boo, or a stolen remote control.

He had shown us what love really looks like, and it wasn't always pretty. Sometimes love was holding a screaming baby at 3 a.m. with spit-up on my shirt and mismatched socks on my feet. Sometimes it was cheering for a burp like it was an Olympic medal.

So we decided, we're celebrating.

We invited everyone we knew. Booked a small hall. Filled it with balloons, laughter, and the faint smell of sugar-overload. It wasn't Pinterest-perfect, but it was perfect for us.

And oh, he owned the party. He ran around, chased balloons like they were rare treasures, and attacked his cake with the enthusiasm of a tiny dessert-destroying Godzilla. The cake ended up on his face, in his hair, on the tablecloth, and mysteriously on every human that picked him to cuddle that day.

Did he understand what was happening? Probably not.
Did we? Absolutely.

This wasn't just a birthday party.
It was our victory lap.
It was proof that we had not only survived the first year, we had thrived in it.

Reflections & Lessons

- You can't always prevent the fall, but you can be there to pick them up. That fall in the walker reminded me I didn't need to be a superhero, I just needed to be calm, loving, present… and fast.
- When they begin to walk, they also begin to walk away. And that's hard. The first steps aren't just physical, they're emotional. They mark the beginning of little separations… and the beginning of trust.
- Celebrate even if they won't remember it. Because *you* will. The first birthday is not just about your baby. It's about how far you've come. That joy deserves to be honoured.
- Letting go doesn't mean abandoning. It means believing they're ready, and you are too, even if you don't feel like it.
- Motherhood keeps evolving, and so do you. The first year is just the foundation. Every new stage will demand a new version of you. Somehow, you'll keep showing up, stronger, softer, wiser.

- You'll feel like you're doing everything wrong… until your baby laughs. That laugh is proof you're doing something very right.
- Your baby isn't asking for perfection, they're asking for you. Show up as the real you, cake-smeared, hair-messy, and heart-wide-open.
- Some days you'll lead. Some days you'll follow. Some days you'll just hold hands through the storm. All of it counts. All of it matters.
- Comparison is a thief. No one else is raising your baby, so their milestones, their party, their pace… none of it has to match anyone else's.
- The smallest moments become the most sacred. That quiet cuddle after the chaos? That's the real gift.

21

FIRST GOODBYE TO BABYHOOD: THE RETURN TO WORK EDITION

As his first birthday loomed, a new challenge surfaced, and this time, it wasn't about him.
It was about me.

I wanted to go back to work. I was missing the outside world chaos!

Now, this wasn't just about stepping out of the house in a freshly ironed kurta and pretending I still had an adult life. No. This was about letting go, even if just for a few hours a day.

It meant handing my baby over to someone else. Someone who wouldn't know his tiny "I'm hungry but pretending I'm not" face. Someone who might not notice the microscopic signs of an impending meltdown. Someone who, frankly, might not leap across the room like a Bollywood stunt double to catch him mid-fall.

And so… separation anxiety.
For both of us.

I began my search like a mum on a mission, which, to be fair, is exactly what I was. I interrogated day-care owners like a suspicious police detective.

"How many babies per caregiver?"
"What's your emergency plan?"
"Do you know how to sing 'Twinkle Twinkle' in at least two languages?"

I asked friends, family, neighbours, random parents at the park, even the lady who sells vegetables on the corner. Eventually, we found a day-care that looked warm, welcoming, and full of smiles. I exhaled. This could work.

We enrolled him.

The first few days were… rough. My husband took on drop-off duty. And let me tell you, this man deserves a medal. He listened to our son's heart-wrenching cries every morning, kissed him goodbye at the gate, and walked away. I don't know how he did it without crumbling into a heap on the footpath. I, on the other hand, stayed home listening to phantom cries and pacing the hall like I was outside an emergency surgery procedure.

But slowly, painfully slowly, our son adjusted.

And then one day, I arrived early to pick him up. I thought I'd surprise him, scoop him up, and have one of those joyous slow-motion reunion moments you see in TV ads. Instead, what I saw was the stuff of a mother's nightmares: mess, carelessness, inattentiveness. Not just "we've had a busy morning" messy, no, this was "I've lost faith in humanity" messy.

My stomach dropped. My trust shattered. I knew, with absolute clarity, he was never coming back here again.

And so began The Search: Part Two, this time for a nanny.
Someone kind.
Someone reliable.
Someone who didn't see babies as background noise.

We found her. A warm, loving woman who looked after my son like he was her own. My shoulders dropped for the first time in weeks.

And then… I went back to work.

Walking out that first morning felt like I was leaving my heart behind with a smiley sticker on it. But I did it. And in that moment, I realised something big: letting go is not abandoning. It's trusting. It's believing your baby is okay, and so are you.

Looking back, the first year was more than milestones. It was the story of three people learning from each other, him, me, and his father. It was about building trust, surviving chaos, and finding joy in messes.

The first birthday wasn't the end of a chapter. It was the prologue to the rest of our lives together.

We had not only survived the first year. We had thrived.

I thought the first year was about teaching him how to live, but it turned out, he was teaching me how to be alive.

Reflections & Lessons, First Goodbye to Babyhood

- Separation anxiety is real, for both of you. Don't let anyone tell you to "just get over it." It's a process.
- Day-care tours are like blind dates. Some look great in theory, but you'll know pretty quickly if it's a match.
- Drop-off duty should go to the emotionally tougher partner. And yes, it's perfectly fine to nominate them without discussion.
- Trust is everything. If your gut says "no," listen to it, and act fast.
- A good caregiver is gold. They don't just look after your child; they give you back your peace of mind.
- Going back to work isn't leaving your baby. It's showing them you can be a mother *and* a whole person.
- You're allowed to cry in the car. Then you're allowed to go get yourself a coffee and feel proud you made it out the door.
- Goodbyes get easier. Until the day they wave you off without looking up from their toys, and you'll find yourself missing the clingy phase you once wished away.

PART I: THE FOUNDATION, SURVIVING THE FIRST WEEK

Journal Prompts

- What was your first thought when you saw your baby?
- How did your body feel in those early hours? What do you wish someone had told you about this phase?
- Write a letter to your baby from the hospital bed. What do you want them to know about their birth?

☑ Mini Checklist

PART II: BUILDING THE BOND, FIRST THREE MONTHS

Journal Prompts

- When did I first feel like a "real parent"?
- What moment of overwhelm surprised me?
- How did I care for myself, even in small ways?
- Write about the first time your baby smiled, cooed, or made you laugh.

☑ Mini Checklist

____

____

____

____

____

____

PART III: GROWING TOGETHER, 3 TO 8 MONTHS

Journal Prompts

- What sound or expression from my baby melted me completely?
- Describe a mess that turned into a memory.
- What emotion have I had to welcome, rather than resist?
- When did I feel the first signs of confidence?

☑ Mini Checklist

____

____

____

____

____

____

PART IV: THE LEAP, 8 TO 12 MONTHS

Journal Prompts

- What was my baby's bravest moment this month?
- How did I support them through a scary fall, fever, or frustration?
- When did I last feel like I was "doing okay", and meant it?
- Write a letter to your baby on their first birthday.

☑ Mini Checklist

____

____

____

____

____

____